A
Spy's Guide
To
Taking Risks

by

John Braddock

For updates on next books, join the email list at:

www.spysguide.com

Contents

1

Thinking About Risks

When the truck crashed into my taxi, I wasn't ready.

I should have been ready. I knew cars malfunction. I knew weather makes roads slippery. I knew drivers make bad decisions. I knew there was a chance of a crash because I'd seen them before. And been in one myself. I knew a crash was a possibility before I got in the taxi.

But I didn't think a crash was probable. I didn't think it was likely.

Plus, I was thinking about other risks.

I was thinking about how to get safely and securely to a meeting with a sensitive source. I was thinking about how to handle the meeting, since the source

---

was a volatile guy.

And I was thinking about the people who were hunting me.

When you're a spy, surveillance teams and state security and the Border Patrol are using cell phone telemetry and drones and people on the ground to follow you. They're trying to surveil you without you knowing, so they can stop you and arrest you or worse.

To escape them, you sometimes travel in alias. Which is a different set of risks. Travelling in alias means you can be arrested for anything. State security doesn't need an excuse to arrest you. All they need to do is to stop you, and it's over.

And something else that day made it riskier: It was my first time traveling in alias.

The first time you do anything, it's hard to make probability judgments. You don't know all that's possible, much less what's probable. You don't know all the causal factors and you haven't seen all the effects. You don't know what to watch for. Which means you don't how to react. The first time you do anything, there's a higher risk of failure.

But when you're a spy, your job is to take risks. Your job is to figure out what's possible, reason backward and make probability judgments. Your job is to get intelligence without the other side knowing you have it. Even while they're hunting you.

Your job is to take risks.

The source I would meet that day had intelligence that was making a difference in the wars we were fighting.

Getting it was worth the risks.

Those were the risks I was thinking of when I got in the taxi.

I wasn't thinking about the risk of a car crash.

Even so, I should have put on my seatbelt.

When I knocked on the passenger window of his taxi, the driver jumped out and met me at the rear.

Most taxi drivers are settled in. Relaxed. Their minds and bodies calmed by hours of waiting.

Not this guy. He was hyped up. He was frantic. He was jumpy. Like he might be on a drug. Maybe, the local amphetamine.

In the local language, he asked where I was going.

The train station, I told him.

He put a hand on my roller bag. I gave it to him, which turned out to be a mistake. He shoved the bag in the trunk. I slid onto the leather backseat.

The driver's seat had wooden beads for blood circulation. The rearview mirror had hanging charms. The dashboard gaps held pieces of paper. Like a lot of taxi drivers, he was running a business on the side. Which was normal.

The taxi driver sprinted back to his door. Squishing the wooden beads to turn sideways, the driver asked again, "The train station?"

I had just told him that, and he was asking again. If I wasn't distracted by looking out the back window for surveillance, I would have taken that as a bad sign. But I didn't.

I said, Yes, the train station.

____

The driver accelerated into a traffic circle. He was driving fast, but not crazy fast. Not out-of-the-ordinary fast for a taxi driver in this part of the world.

As we went around the inner ring of the traffic circle, I watched out the back window for anything that could signal surveillance. Like someone on foot jumping into a van. Or someone going from a van to a taxi. Or unrelated people suddenly congregating. I was watching for what surveillance teams do when they don't think anyone is watching.

There was nothing.

The driver completed a circle and passed the taxi stand. Which was strange. A full circle, instead of going toward the train station.

He was going fast in the inner ring of traffic. The outer ring of traffic was moving slow. He turned toward an exit.

A truck in the outer ring came across the exit.

Maybe the taxi driver thought his car was faster than it was. Maybe he thought the truck was slower than it was. Or maybe he was playing chicken. Maybe, he didn't care.

Either way, the taxi driver accelerated. The truck accelerated, too.

The taxi driver cut across the front of the truck and gunned it.

It wasn't enough.

Before a low-probability event like a car crash happens, it's just an idea. It's just an imagined thing. It's just a statistic.

Then it happens.

Metal crunches. Plastic shatters. Your body was going one way. Now, it's going another.

Like the shock from an explosion, your organs shift. You move in unexpected ways. If you're not wearing a seatbelt, you go somewhere else.

I flew across the leather seat. My shoulder slammed into the far door.

The car landed half-on, half off the median.

A moment of quiet. Then curses from the taxi

driver in a language that wasn't the local language.

He turned and said, "It's okay. Stay here, sir."

He got out and looked at the taxi's banged up rear.

The truck driver got out and looked at the truck's banged up front.

Then, the screaming started.

Neither driver was a local, but the screams sounded like a common language. Maybe they had the same home country. Or shared a border. Maybe they were old ethnic enemies. Maybe their people had been screaming at each other for centuries.

Whatever the history of their peoples, they screamed and yelled with words I didn't know.

I started thinking about a risk more serious than a car crash for a spy on his first day in alias: That the police were on their way.

When you first encounter risk, it's a feeling.

It's being at the top of a slide. It's seeing a snake in the grass. It's a wave pushing you under. It's your gut telling you something is about to go very bad.

If you get past it, there's another feeling: Exhilaration. You go down the slide, escape the snake and come up for air. You feel relief. Because the worst didn't happen. You survived.

Then, you take a statistics class or talk to a financial planner or get a medical checkup, and they tell you risk is something different.

Risk isn't a feeling, they say. Risk is large numbers. Risk is modeling and sample sizes and variance and projections of the future. The professor, analyst, or doctor say risk is too complicated for your gut. They say your gut will steer you wrong.

They tell you to trust the large numbers. They tell you data has been collected and categorized and analyzed and turned into probabilities and confidence intervals. They tell you smart people have used complicated computations to figure out risks. They say to trust the experts. The experts will

---

tell you the risks to take.

Then you become a spy, and risk becomes a feeling again.

The fear returns. The dread is back. The pit in your stomach, too. You're on top of a cliff and looking over the edge every day.

Despite the fear, you stay on the edge. You take the risks because there's no other way to get what your side needs. There's no other way to stop worse things from happening. There's no other way to get the intelligence that stops a terrorist attack, saves lives or stops a war.

But you want to take smart risks. You want to avoid mistakes. You want to do the mission and get back safely, so you can take risks another day.

To take smart risks, you go back to what the large numbers guys told you. You go back to the modeling and sample sizes and calculations of variance and projections of the future. You look for tools you can use as a spy.

Tools you can use when risk is a feeling. When risk is fear, dread and a pit in your stomach. Tools you can you use when you're under stress and thinking quickly. Tools that help you take smart risks.

You look for tools that are simple. Tools that are reliable. Tools that are time-tested.

And they need to fit in your head.

When you're a spy in the field, you can't run regressions. You don't have algorithms and statistical tests. You don't even have a calculator, most of the time. You can't rely on large numbers.

You need simple tools to help you take smart risks.

When you go out in alias, the police, Border Patrol and security services are looking for you. They want to arrest you. Or kill you. They're hunting you.

You become the prey.

And not just you. They're hunting the people giving you intelligence, too. They're hunting your sources. Which means the security services will surveil you, if they can. They'll follow you to the meeting or the brush pass or the dead drop so they can arrest or kill your source.

Your source takes a risk to get you the intelligence. You take a risk because there's no other way to know what an enemy is planning. You both take risks because there's no other way to stop a terrorist attack or win a war or confound an enemy action.

When you become prey, you do what all prey does: You keep moving.

Before the taxi crash, I had a plan for my day, built from the end backwards.

The destination was a medium-sized town. A town big enough the locals wouldn't be suspicious of outsiders. And small enough there wouldn't be a lot of surveillance.

A good town for a spy to meet a source.

To get there, I worked backward. I built a plan with stops, transportation changes and chokepoints. Then a train across a border and more stops, changes and chokepoints.

It was a plan that would give me lots of chances to detect surveillance, if surveillance was on me.

The first part of the day went according to plan. I took on who I would be.

New documentation. New shirts but old pants I didn't wear anymore. New underwear. Shoes just for this identity. What I didn't wear was tucked in my roller bag, anonymously purchased.

A new me with a new name.

The new me traveled around. The new me went through different parts of town. Where it was natural to make transportation changes. Where it was natural to go through chokepoints. Where I could detect surveillance, if surveillance was on me.

After an hour, I didn't think surveillance was on me. But that was just a hypothesis. A hypothesis to test over and over again.

I was at the taxi stand an hour before my train would leave. In normal traffic, the train station was ten minutes away. Plenty of time to get there. Plenty of time to buy a ticket and get on the train. But not so much time that I would be sitting too long in the train station. I was prey and wanted to keep moving.

Then the crash. Which meant I stopped moving. I was in a taxi, half-on and half-off the median. With the two drivers screaming at each other. With the police probably on the way.

The police would be friendly, at first. They'd ask what I saw. They'd take down my statement. They'd ask to see my false documents. They'd ask questions about who I was. About where I was going. About why I was there. Then they'd want contact information, so they could follow up later.

All of which I'd give them.

None of which would be true.

Which would probably be fine. Because I was trained to talk to the police in non-alerting ways. But talking to the police was riskier than not talking to the police. And I would be doing it for the first time in alias.

More importantly, talking to the police would keep me from moving.

I had a plan to follow. I had a source to meet. And I was prey. I wanted to keep moving.

Then, the screaming stopped. The taxi driver came back to the taxi.

He was breathing hard like his heart was racing. Maybe from screaming at the truck driver. Or maybe from the local amphetamine. "Everything is fine," he said. "Just a bump."

It was more than a bump. It was a crash, with crunched metal and shattered plastic. But if he thought it was just a bump, fine with me. As long as we kept moving.

The driver pulled off the curb. He accelerated back into traffic. Not as aggressively this time.

We went 200 yards to a red light and stopped. The taxi driver was still breathing hard. I was still thinking about what happened. Thinking about the risks.

Then, tires screeched behind us.

It was the truck that had just slammed into us.

The truck driver jumped out. He ran to the taxi

---

driver's door. With one hand, he pulled the driver's door open, grabbed the driver's shirt and pulled him out. His other hand had his phone at his ear.

The truck driver yelled that he had the police on the phone.

Worse, he yelled it in the local language.

Which meant he was yelling it to me.

Which meant he wanted me to know the police were coming. He wanted me to talk to the police.

A few hours into my first day in alias, the police were coming to interview me about a car crash.

It was time to react to the risk.

When you think of risks, you think about probabilities. The first people to think about probabilities were thinking about games.

It started with throwing the astragali, rolling the dice and spinning the roulette wheel. In games like those, you know all the possibilities. The astragali bones can turn up only so many ways. A die can show only one of six sides. On an American roulette wheel, the ball can land in only one of 38 places.

Knowing all the possibilities means you can calculate the probabilities of random events. On a six-sided die, it's a one in six chance that any one number comes up, or 16.67%. On an American roulette wheel, the probability any single number gets the ball is 1 out of 38, or 2.6%.

If you did that kind of probability analysis for spies, you'd start with the possibilities. And you'd gather them from history.

In the history of espionage, a lot of bad things have happened to spies. Some spies have been surveilled and exposed. Some spies have been arrested and killed. Some spies have seen their people subjugated and killed, which is worse than death.

But good things have happened, too. Some spies have saved lives. Some spies have won wars. Some spies have stopped wars from happening. Some spies have saved the world.

If you categorized all the historical data, turned them into possibilities and put them on a scale of bad to good, it might look like this:

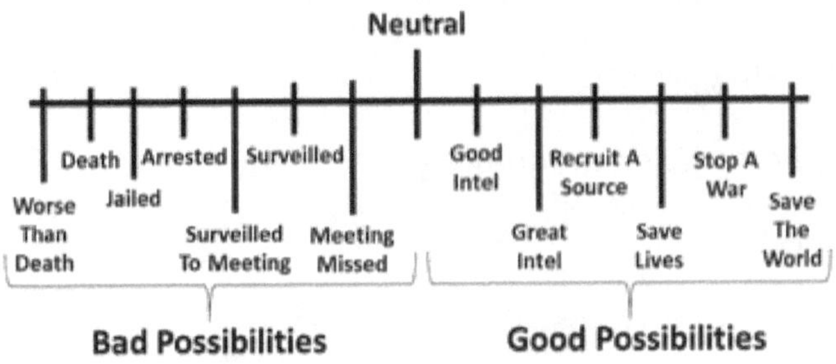

On the good side are:

1. Collecting good intelligence.

2. Collecting great, actionable intelligence.

3. Recruiting a new source of intelligence.

4. Saving lives.

5. Stopping or winning wars.

6. Saving the world.

On the bad side are:

1. Missing a meeting with a source.

2. Being identified as a spy and surveilled.

3. Being surveilled to a meeting.

4. Being arrested.

5. Being jailed indefinitely.

6. Death.

7. Worse than death.

If those were 100 percent of the things that could happen, the next step would be counting how many times each thing happened. You'd get the quantity or frequency of each category.

When you tallied them up, the result might look like this:

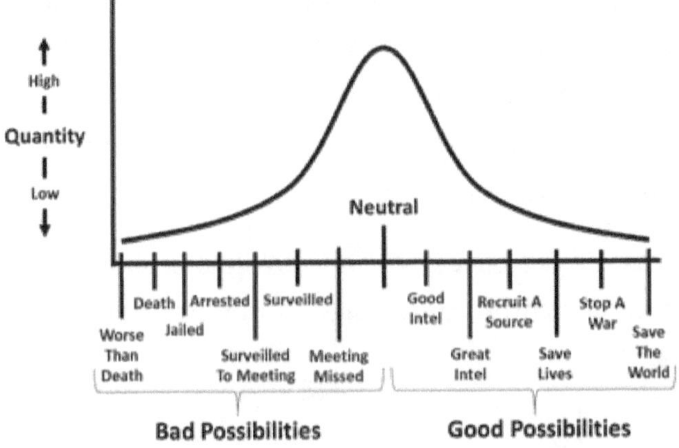

It might be that most events are clustered around neutral. You might see fewer events as you get to the extremes on either side. It might look like a normal curve around a neutral mean. You might see relatively few events on the extremes. You might see relatively few deaths of spies. You might also see relatively few times a spy saved the world. You might see a symmetry between good and bad results.

Maybe.

If you did, then you could apply statistical tools.

You could calculate mean and variance and standard deviations. You could say that across the full population of spy-days in history, surveillance has happened on five percent of those days. On less than one percent of those days, a spy has saved lives. On the other side, maybe .09 percent of those days, a spy is killed.

Or maybe the curve doesn't look like that. Maybe the curve is more to the right and narrower, like this:

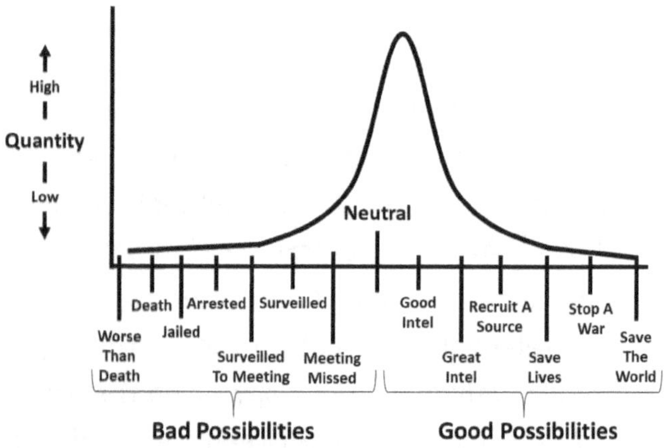

Which means the probabilities are different.

Or maybe the curve is bimodal, like this:

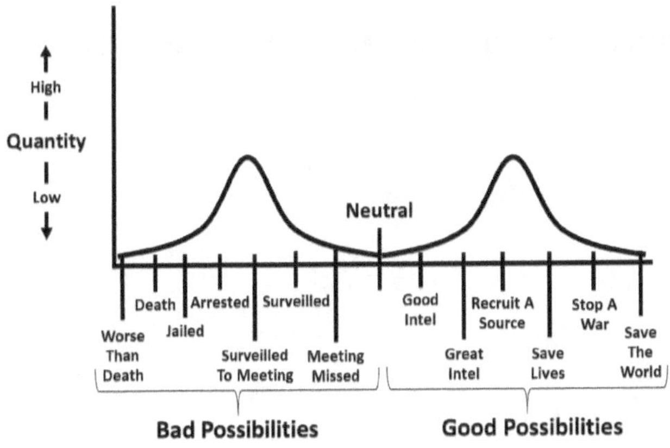

Which means the probabilities are different again.

The shape of the curve is good to know, if you're leader of a country or head of a spy agency or a chief of station.

If you have a job like that, you're making decisions about large numbers. Large numbers of spies and large numbers of events. You're thinking about cumulative effects and averages. You can afford to have a few spies exposed or arrested or worse, because you've got plenty more.

But when you're a spy in the field, you can't rely on

large numbers.

Which means you think about risk differently.

2

Seeing Risks

The truck driver had the taxi driver's shirt balled up in his hand. He had his back against my door. Like he was trying to keep me from opening it.

But he hadn't done anything about the door on the other side.

My options were:

1. Stay in the taxi and talk to the police; or

2. Keep moving.

I didn't want to talk to the police. And being prey, I wanted to keep moving.

I took Option 2.

I slid across the leather seat and pushed open the far door.

The stoplight turned green. Traffic tried to move around us. Horns sounded behind the truck.

That's when I realized my earlier mistake.

At the taxi stand, I let the taxi driver put my roller bag in the trunk. The trunk that had been smashed by the truck in the crash.

I didn't know if the crash had damaged the latch. I didn't know if the trunk would open.

The truck driver hadn't noticed me get out the other side. He was shouting over the horns to the police dispatcher on the phone. He didn't see me feel for the trunk release.

To get my bag out of the trunk, two things had to happen next. Not one, but both. Getting my bag out of the trunk had two necessary conditions:

1. The latch had to be undamaged; and

2. The trunk had to be unlocked.

If I were to guess at the probabilities for both, they would be:

1. That the latch hadn't been damaged: 30%.

2. That the trunk wasn't locked: 50%.

Thirty percent on the latch because the truck had hit us hard. Hard enough to push metal and damage the lock mechanism.

Fifty percent on the trunk not being locked because the driver was too frantic for details like locking trunks. But there could be an automatic lock. So, 50% that the trunk was locked.

Because both things had to happen to get my bag, that meant multiplying the two probabilities together: .3 multiplied by .5. That equaled a 15% chance that the trunk would open.

Not high. Either way, I was going to walk away. Plus or minus my roller bag. Plus or minus my new shirts, old pants and new underwear.

I found the trunk release and pressed it.

It opened. A small miracle.

I pulled out my bag. Closed the trunk door softly.

Though he was just a couple of feet away, the truck driver didn't turn around.

But the taxi driver was facing me and watching. He smiled ruefully and half-shrugged. Half-shrugged because he couldn't do a full shrug while his shirt was held by the truck driver.

I thought about throwing some money on the seat. But the taxi driver only took me a few hundred yards. And he crashed into a truck. So I didn't.

I pulled my bag through traffic. Another horn blast from a frustrated driver, and I was at the sidewalk.

That's when the truck driver turned and saw me. He shouted. Told me to stop.

I kept walking.

Which meant the truck driver's choices were:

1. Chase after me; or

2. Hold on to the taxi driver.

He couldn't do both.

He had to weigh the probabilities, along with the possible results.

If he chased after me, there was a high probability the taxi driver would drive away. Plus, there was a high probability I would get away. He had to weigh the benefits of chasing me against the probability of losing the taxi driver.

The truck driver made his choice: He held on to the

taxi driver. He yelled again at me but didn't chase
me.

I didn't want him to change his mind, so I took the
first set of stairs near the sidewalk. Which took me
underground. Into a subway station.

A subway car was arriving. Lit up on the front was
the name of my train station.

What were the chances of that? Low, it seemed to
me.

Which meant I had benefited from two low-
probability events right after the taxi crash: The
trunk latch working and a subway arriving to take
me to the train station.

My first day in alias was getting better, I thought.

But I was wrong.

When you're a spy in the field, you're working with
small numbers. A small number of spies and
sources and a small number of events. Most of the

time you're working with the smallest number of all: One.

You're thinking about the one game someone is playing with you. Hopefully, a Positive-Sum Game. Sometimes, a Zero-Sum Game.

You're thinking about the one meeting you're going to have. You're thinking about the one source you're going to meet.

You're thinking about the one piece of intelligence you want to get.

And you're thinking about what can happen if you do one thing wrong.

One bad decision can ruin you. One mistake means you're exposed or arrested or worse. One exposure or arrest, and it's over. One wrong step in some places, and you're dead.

When you're working with small numbers, you can't get one wrong.

You can't lose a few and recoup the losses later. You can't spread your bets. You're all-in every time you walk out the door or get in a taxi or get on a train. You can't afford failure.

When you're working with small numbers, you don't take risks the way the people with large numbers do.

When you're a spy, you make decisions about risks differently.

You start by building a simple model.

In firefighter training, the first thing they teach you is a simple model for fire.

In the simple model of fire, you start with what's necessary for a fire to exist. It takes three things:

1. Fuel; and

2. Oxygen; and

3. Heat

The simple model looks like this:

Fuel & Oxygen & Heat = Fire

A fire needs all three to exist. If one of them is missing, the fire won't exist.

But there are different kinds of fuel. And different ways to get oxygen. And different sources of heat.

Underneath each of the necessary conditions are factors you can substitute for other factors.

For fuel, there are liquids, gases and solids. There are so many of each, they've been put into classes. For oxygen, there's air and oxidizing agents. For heat, there are flames, friction, hot surfaces and other sources. Underneath the necessary conditions are substitutes.

If you put them all together, it looks like this:

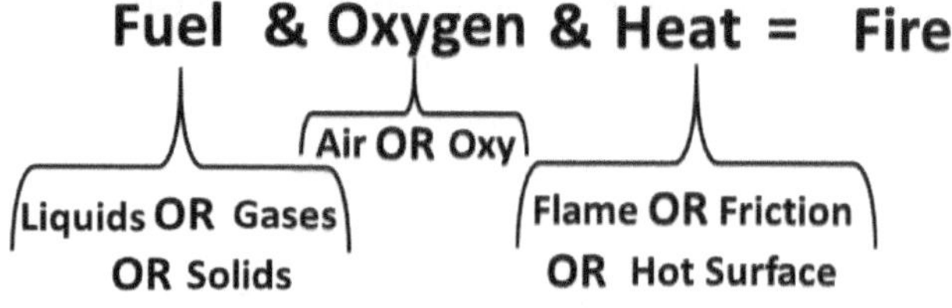

At the top of the simple model are the necessary conditions of a fire, connected by & operators. Underneath each are the substitute factors, connected by OR operators.

The rest of firefighter training is figuring out how to take away one of the necessary conditions and survive.

Remove all of the fuel, and you won't have a fire, even if oxygen and heat are there:

Remove oxygen, and the fire goes out, even if fuel and heat are there:

Remove heat, and there's no more fire, even if fuel and oxygen are there:

Fuel, oxygen and heat are each a necessary condition of a fire. Without one of them, there is no fire.

This simple model tells a firefighter a lot of things.

———————————————

It tells a firefighter about cause and effect. It tells a firefighter about the relationship between precursors. Most importantly, it tells the firefighter how to make sure a fire doesn't exist.

When you're a spy, there are a lot of things you don't want to exist.

You don't want terrorist attacks to exist. You don't want invasions to exist. When you're in alias in a foreign country, you don't want surveillance to exist.

To stop them from existing, you build a simple model for each one.

You figure out the necessary conditions for each bad thing that can happen. And the substitutes underneath.

Which is why firefighter training is a little like spy training. Except spy instructors don't give you the simple model to stop a bad thing from happening.

Spy instructors don't tell you the necessary conditions. They don't tell you every cause and effect. They don't tell you the relationship between precursors. They don't tell you which piece to remove to stop a terrorist attack or an invasion or surveillance from happening.

They don't tell you because they can't.

They can't tell you because the causes and effects are always changing.

Which means spy instructors back up a step. Before they teach you how to handle risks, they teach you how to construct simple models of the world.

They do that by telling you stories.

Spy instructors tell you what happened to them in a certain place and a certain time. They tell you how they detected surveillance in a dangerous place. They tell you how they escaped with important intelligence. They tell you how they stopped a terrorist attack. Or didn't.

They tell you what they saw. They tell you the decisions they made. They tell you the actions they took. They tell you how they survived. And they tell you the stories of other spies who didn't.

With their stories, you build your first simple models of how espionage works. How one thing connects to another. How things you may think are uncertain happen repeatedly. How things you would think are a sure thing happen rarely. How random events intervene and change outcomes.

You build your first simple models of cause and effect.

Then, you role-play situations, and you learn to build simple models on the fly.

You take in data and analyze it to find causes and effects.

You generate hypotheses and test them.

You identify the necessary conditions of bad things. You identify the substitutes. You identify the & operators. You identify the OR operators.

You build simple models on the fly.

Plus, you do it in the middle of risky situations. You do it while being afraid and sweaty and tired and exhausted.

The model building starts with identifying necessary conditions.

In the subway car, my train station's name was illuminated on the front. After the unlucky car crash, I felt lucky again.

But I still faced the risk of surveillance.

To analyze that risk, I built a simple model in my head. A simple model of what it would take for a surveillance team to be on me.

To be on me, a surveillance team would have had to follow me from the beginning of the day through jumping into the taxi, through the crash and into the subway car. And they would need to be watching me without me spotting them.

Each step was a necessary condition for surveillance to be on me.

The simple model looked like this:

Beginning of the Day	&	Jumping in the Taxi	&	Through the Crash	&	Into the Subway	=	Surveillance on Me

The next step was to put probabilities on each one.

In the mid-2000s, Iran was acting suspiciously. Some U.S. decision-makers thought Iran was building a nuclear weapon. Others thought they weren't.

The U.S. National Intelligence Council was told to come up with the answer. In 2007, they produced a National Intelligence Estimate (NIE) to answer the question.

It was a dangerous time for the U.S. Intelligence Community. After getting wrong the 2002 National Intelligence Estimate on Iraq's Weapons of Mass Destruction, the Intelligence Community couldn't afford another failure.

When the NIE on the Iranian nuclear weapons program came out in 2007, there was a special section that wasn't in previous NIEs. The section was called, "What We Mean When We Say: An Explanation Of Estimative Language."

It said:

"We use phrases such as we judge, we assess, and we estimate—and probabilistic terms such as probably and likely—to convey analytical assessments and judgments. Such statements are not facts, proof, or knowledge . . . Because analytical judgments are not certain, we use probabilistic language to reflect the Community's estimates of the likelihood of developments or events."

The section included a chart that put "probabilistic language" on a scale. It looked like this:

Remote	Very unlikely	Unlikely	Even chance	Probably/ Likely	Very likely	Almost certainly

They wanted to be clear: When talking about probabilities for the single event of Iran getting a nuclear weapon, they didn't mean the kind of top-down probabilities you get from frequency distributions or sampling or large numbers.

They were talking about probabilities built on knowledge about cause and effect.

Those probabilities weren't "facts, proof or knowledge."

Which meant those probabilities were estimates and guesses.

Guesses informed by intelligence from sensitive sources.

But guesses all the same.

So why bother?

Why bother with a report full of guesses? Why bother with probability judgments at all?

Because there was something else that the probability judgments showed. Something more important than the probability judgments themselves.

The probability judgments showed a simple model. A simple model of cause and effect.

In the "Key Judgments" section of the 2007 NIE, the National Intelligence Council laid out a simple model for the Iranians getting a nuclear weapon.

But they didn't lay it out in an easy-to-read model form. They didn't put the causal factors on the left and an "equals" sign and the effect on the right.

Instead, they listed the factors that affected their probability judgments:

1. Intent of Iranian leadership

____

2. Importation of a nuclear weapon

3. Importation of weapons-usable fissile material

4. Internal creation of weapons-usable fissile material

5. Scientific and technical ability to create a nuclear weapon

Were some of these necessary conditions for the Iranians to get a nuclear weapon? Were some substitutes for other factors? How would the factors interact to produce an Iranian nuclear weapon?

When you laid out the simple model of cause and effect, you saw exactly how the Iranians could get a nuclear weapon.

For the risk of surveillance, I had a simple model of cause and effect.

A surveillance team would have had to follow me from the beginning of the day through jumping into the taxi, through the crash and into the subway car. And they would need to be watching me without me spotting them.

Now, it was time to put probabilities on them.

The probabilities were estimates. The probabilities were guesses. Guesses informed by my limited experience. Guesses informed by the stories I'd heard. Guesses informed by my training. But guesses all the same.

They were probabilities for single events. Events which wouldn't be repeated. Which meant the probabilities couldn't be tested. The probabilities couldn't be refined over time.

My guesses at probabilities were either right or they were wrong. But they were still useful.

My guesses at the probabilities of surveillance being on me without me seeing them were:

1. At the beginning of the day: 10%

2. Through jumping in the taxi: 5%

3. If they somehow followed me through jumping in the taxi, that they followed me through the crash: 80%

4. If the previous three, they followed me into the subway car: 20%

Those were guesses. But because each one was a necessary condition of surveillance still on me as I sat in the subway car, I multiplied the probabilities together: .08%. One chance in 1,250.

Which meant the bottom-up probability of being followed was low. It was remote. But the probability wasn't zero.

Then, there was another risk: The risk that I had attracted new attention. The risk that a surveillance team hadn't been on me at the beginning of the day, but something I had done attracted their attention. That a surveillance team had jumped on me now.

But that was nearly impossible. To do that, a surveillance team would have been stationed in the area, not already on someone else and able to re-orient themselves to me. The odds of that were remote.

But the odds weren't zero.

The subway car made a turn. And then another turn. The turns felt like we were going away from the train station.

I scrambled to a map.

The map said the same thing that was lit up on the front of the subway car: The destination was the train station. But first, we would go in a giant loop. We would go all over the city before reaching the train station.

Which was a problem. With the crash and the drivers screaming at each other and the second stop, some of the time I planned for travel had been used up. Now, we were going in the wrong direction.

A new risk: I wouldn't make it on time to take the train across the border. If I missed that train, I would miss the next train on the other side of the border. Which would mean missing the meeting. It was a border crossing and half a day away but missing that first train meant missing the meeting.

Which meant my plan was a bad plan. It had a single point of failure. No fallback. No substitute underneath. No OR operator for missing that first train. No other way to make the meeting, if I missed it.

My bad plan to get to the meeting looked like this:

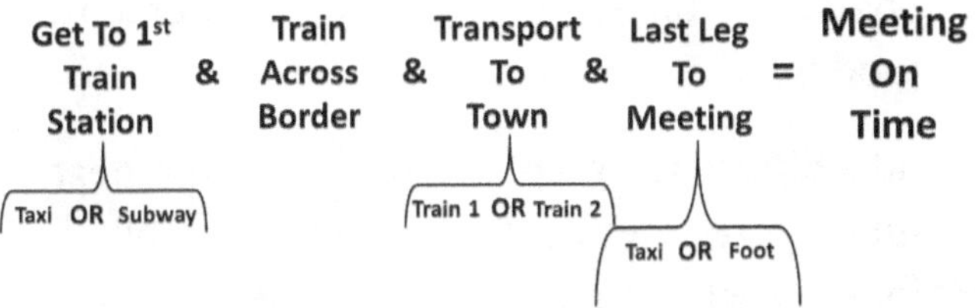

If I didn't make the meeting, I'd miss the documents the source had risked bringing that day. If his intelligence was time-sensitive, it would lose its value. Plus, my first day in alias in a foreign country would be for nothing. All that risk for nothing.

But I hadn't missed the train across the border yet. Which meant there were more OR operators to play with.

I looked at the subway map again. Compared it to the above ground map in my head.

If I got out, I'd need to find a taxi quickly. Maybe a 40 percent chance I could find one in time. Then there was the chance the taxi would get me to the train station in time. Maybe 20 percent.

Both had to happen, which meant & operators. Which meant multiplying the two together. Odds of making the train station with a taxi above ground: .40 multiplied by .20, which is 8 percent. Not good odds.

So I did a different kind of math. I timed the next two subway stops and extrapolated. I multiplied the time of each stop by the number of stops and factored in the time between stops.

The result: Three minutes. The subway would arrive at the train station three minutes before my train would leave, if my math was right and the subway stayed on schedule.

At the train station, there would be a long flight of stairs to climb. Then 100 yards to the train platform. Then a ticket booth. Where I'd need to get a ticket.

Because I didn't have a ticket. I didn't have a ticket to lower the risk of another bad thing happening: Security services finding out where I was going.

Without a ticket on me, my destination wouldn't be known, if I was arrested. Without a ticket, security services wouldn't know where I was going. Which lowered the risk of my source being caught, if I was arrested.

Now, being without a ticket was a problem for me.

When I got to the train station, I had a lot to do in three minutes, if I was going to make the train.

That three minutes was if the subway was on time, and I didn't know the probability of that.

Somebody somewhere had data on the reliability of public transportation services in this town. They'd probably isolated the factors that drove reliability of various routes and could adjust by hour of the day, weather conditions and day of the week. They could predict how close to on-time my subway car would be.

But I didn't have the data. I didn't know the & and OR operators that drove on-time reliability in this town. Which meant I couldn't even make an informed guess.

So I did the next-best thing, even though it wasn't a very good thing: I compared this city to other cities like it and my experience on the subway systems of those cities.

It wasn't a great way to do it, but I had nothing better.

I guessed the subway car would get to the train

station on time with an 80 percent probability.

Which was a lot higher than the 8 percent probability if I left and tried to find a taxi.

I stayed on the subway car.

Fortunately, the subway had no delays at that hour of the day on that route with those weather conditions. We arrived at the train station three minutes before my train was scheduled to leave.

I took the stairs two at a time. At the top was a gate. I pushed through and sprinted.

Half rolling, half bouncing my bag, I charged through the train station crowd.

I saw the ticket booth.

It had a long line.

Which meant there was a new calculation to make.

But this one was simple: if I waited in line at the ticket booth, it would take longer than the one minute I had left. It would mean a 100 percent chance of missing the train.

I ran past the ticket booth to the train platform. On the platform was an official with a ticket machine slung over his shoulder.

Breathing hard, I asked, Can I buy a ticket from you?

"No," he answered. "It's impossible."

Impossible means the probability of an event is zero. That didn't sound right, since he had a ticket machine on his shoulder.

Impossible? I repeated.

"Impossible," he answered. "You must go to the ticket booth and buy a ticket there."

Which meant two options:

1. Go back to the ticket booth and miss the train and miss the meeting; or

2. Jump on the train without a ticket. Which could bring extra scrutiny.

Option 1 meant no good could come of this day. My first day in alias would be a failure. All that risk for nothing.

Option 2 meant the possibility of extra scrutiny. Which meant increasing the probability of getting caught. Which meant taking on more risk.

The train horn sounded.

I made my choice.

In the 2007 National Intelligence Estimate on Iran was a simple model of the risk of the Iranians getting a nuclear weapon. Some of the factors were necessary conditions, like the intent of the Iranian leadership & their capability. Some of the factors were substitutes, like importing a nuclear weapon or creating one internally.

If you built a simple model based on the 2007 NIE's "Key Judgments," it would look like this:

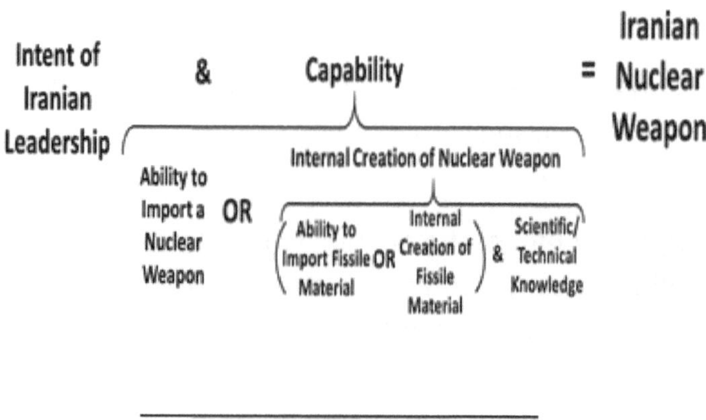

The Iranian leadership needed the will & capability to build a nuclear weapon. But underneath capability were other factors: Either importing a nuclear weapon OR creating one internally.

Importing a nuclear weapon was a substitute for internal creation of a nuclear weapon, and vice versa. They could do one or the other. Which means neither factor was individually a necessary condition. But together they were.

If the Iranian leadership decided to create a nuclear weapon internally, they would need two things: Fissile material and the scientific/technical knowledge to use it in constructing a nuclear weapon. Fissile material and scientific/technical knowledge were necessary conditions for internal creation of a nuclear weapon. But fissile material could either be imported OR created internally, which meant neither importation nor internal creation was a necessary condition.

The simple model of causes for the Iranians getting a nuclear weapon was there in the 2007 NIE, hidden in the probabilities and the "Key Judgments" section of the report.

It was a simple model of necessary conditions and substitutes. A simple model of & operators and the OR operators. Of causes and effect. A logical model.

But the 2007 NIE wasn't just an assessment. With the simple model established, it created a road map for lowering the risk.

To lower the risk, you could affect the intentions of the Iranian leadership with sanctions and diplomatic efforts.

To lower the risk, you could limit the ability of the Iranians to import weapons and highly-enriched uranium.

To lower the risk, you could restrict the tools and instruments used to make fissile material internally.

But lower it how much?

Would taking those steps reduce the risk from 90% to 50%? Would it go from very likely to neutral? Would it go from neutral to unlikely?

It's hard to know.

It's hard to know what the real probabilities of

single events really are.

It's hard to know if something is unlikely, neutral or very likely. It's even harder to know exact probabilities. It's hard to know if the chance of something is 10% or 50% or 90%. And after the fact, it's hard to know, in single events, if you were right.

Which is why you see people in risky situations do something different: Instead of working to lower the risk of a bad thing, they work to remove necessary conditions.

When you remove a necessary condition of a risk, the risk can't exist.

3

Choosing Risks

On the train platform, I chose Option #2.

I jumped on the train without a ticket, even though it could mean extra scrutiny.

I was still sweating from running through the train station when I found the train manager two cars back.

I'm sorry, I said to the train manager. I don't have a ticket. Can I buy one from you?

He looked me up and down and shrugged. "Of course. No problem."

Great, I said.

"Because you are buying on the train, you must pay extra for a normal seat," he said.

Okay, I said.

"Or you can have a first-class seat for the same price," he said.

I can have a coach seat or a first-class seat for the same price? I confirmed.

"Yes," he said.

Okay, I said. I'll take the first-class seat.

Which turned out to be a mistake.

I rolled my bag into the first-class car and found it empty.

Completely empty. Not a single person in the car. Which was strange. Odds were that there would be someone in the first-class car. But there wasn't anyone. It was just me.

I took a seat by the window. My roller bag went on the seat next to me. After almost losing the bag in the taxi, I didn't want it in the rack above me. I didn't want it in the seat across the aisle. I wanted it within reach.

After a few minutes, the adrenaline in my

bloodstream got metabolized. The sweat stopped. My heartrate went down. I went from hot to a little cold.

I thought through what happened. The taxi accident. The truck driver. The subway ride. The sprint to the train.

Sifted through the data. Analyzed it and put it into the simple model of surveillance. So I could answer a question: What was the probability that I was surveilled?

I already had the probability that I was under surveillance into the subway car: 1 in 1,250. And the likelihood that surveillance had picked me up in the subway car for the first time was also remote.

But there was a new possibility: Did I get picked up by surveillance in the train station?

Transportation hubs like train stations, airports and bus depots have cameras, police and security officers. I could have drawn their attention by sprinting across the train station.

But plenty of people are late for trains. Some sprint through train stations. Some skip ticket booths.

Some get on trains without tickets. I might have attracted attention by what I did, but probably not.

The probability that I was picked up by surveillance in the train station was small, but it was higher than zero. Maybe, one out of twenty. Five percent.

Pretty low, I thought as my body cooked off the last of the adrenaline.

Then, the Border Patrol came into the first-class car.

Three of them in uniform.

One sat behind me.

One sat across from me.

One sat in front of me.

They surrounded me.

The Border Patrol agent in front looked me over, and my adrenaline spiked again.

A friend was in a war zone. The kind of war zone where enemies are trying to kill you. The kind of war zone with checkpoints and soldiers. Soldiers who may or may not be friendly. Which means you keep your pistol ready in your lap.

It was a risky place, but killing my friend was going to be hard.

To kill him, an enemy had to meet several necessary conditions. To kill him an enemy needed to:

1. Find him; and

2. Get past the protection on his vehicle; and

3. Kill him before he killed his attackers.

When my friend started out that day, each necessary condition was low probability. It was low probability that an enemy would find him. It was low probability that an enemy would get past the protection on his vehicle. Because some of that protection included bulletproof glass.

Bulletproof glass doesn't mean permanently bulletproof. Bulletproof glass isn't 100 percent

____

probability bulletproof glass.

Bulletproof glass means it will stop the first bullet. Maybe, the second bullet. Less likely, the third bullet. Especially, if the second or third bullet hits where the first bullet hit.

With every bullet that hits bulletproof glass, the probability increases of the next bullet coming through.

My friend was in the passenger seat as his driver pulled up to a checkpoint.

A soldier stepped in front. Left hand raised. Right hand holding an automatic weapon. Trigger finger pointed along the barrel, like soldiers are trained to do.

A second soldier approached the side of the car. My friend rolled down his window and flashed his papers.

The second soldier turned to the soldier in front of the car.

He nodded.

And ran.

Which was a signal to the soldier in front.

Also, a signal to my friend.

"Go!" he yelled to the driver.

The driver hesitated. "What?"

The soldier in front smiled. His weapon came up. His finger fell to the trigger.

"Go!" said my friend again.

His driver was confused. Too confused to put his foot on the pedal. Too confused to go.

The muzzle of the soldier's rifle flashed. Bullets hit the windshield. Spider webs formed. Bullets searched for weak spots in the bulletproof glass.

My friend raised his pistol and pointed it at the webbing windshield. At the smiling soldier beyond.

That's when something strange happened, he told me later. Something he didn't expect.

He'd been trained for this moment. Silhouettes in shoot houses. Center mass over and over. Again and again. Keep shooting until the target goes down. He'd been trained to kill the enemy before the enemy killed him.

But this was his first moment under live fire. The first moment when a real person was shooting at him. The first moment he would shoot back.

The strange thing, he told me later, was that he wanted the bulletproof windshield out of the way.

He wanted the windshield to fall. He wanted the windshield gone.

Because he wasn't thinking about risks. He was thinking about a task. He was thinking about killing the enemy in front of him, as he'd been trained to do.

As time slowed down, he hated the factory workers who made the bulletproof windshield. He hated the technicians who had installed it. He hated the bureaucrats who procured it and signed the paperwork. He hated everyone who had put that windshield in his way. He cursed them all.

But the bulletproof windshield stayed up.

The enemy soldier got a dry pull. He ejected his magazine. Grabbed another.

There was a pause. A long pause as everything happened slowly.

My friend looked at his driver. He was huddled behind the dashboard. Useless.

His pistol still aimed in front, my friend reached his foot across and found the gas pedal. He grabbed the wheel.

He hit the gas.

The enemy soldier had reloaded. Brought his weapon up. Before he could fire, the car was on top of him. The enemy soldier rolled out of the way. He got up and fired his weapon at them again. Missed completely.

Safely down the road, my friend pulled over. He and his driver checked each other for bullet holes. Because sometimes you don't know you're hit. Sometimes, your body keeps going and doesn't tell you something's wrong.

No bullet holes.

Not a scratch.

The checkpoint soldier got it wrong. He should

have shot the engine. Or the wheels.

Not the bulletproof glass on the windshield.

My friend survived.

When he started out that day, it would have taken three low probability events to kill him.

The first low probability event: He would run into a checkpoint manned by an enemy soldier: Maybe 5%

The second low probability event: The enemy would get past the vehicle's protections. Given the enemy soldier's lack of fire control: Maybe 15%. If the weapon were handled by someone more experienced, that probability would be higher.

Plus a third probabilistic event: After the windshield fell, what were the odds my friend killed the shooter before the shooter killed him?

Harder to judge. By the time the windshield fell, the soldier would have lost the advantage of surprise. Which meant who killed whom first would come down to firepower and training.

My friend had the advantage in training. The

____

enemy soldier had the advantage in firepower. Training usually trumps firepower, which meant my colleague had the advantage.

Maybe a 30% chance that the soldier killed my colleague before my colleague killed the soldier.

Not an overwhelming advantage. With all the bullets flying, the enemy soldier could have been lucky.

At the beginning of the day, the risk was low of dying: .2%. Less than a 1% chance because it took at least three low probability events.

Then, he ran into the checkpoint. Which meant the first low probability event had changed from 5% to 100%. Which meant only two necessary conditions were left. The math changed.

After the enemy found him, the chance of my colleague dying went from .2% to 4.5%.

Big change. But still low. Because he still had the windshield between him and the shooter.

If the windshield had given way, his probability of being killed would have risen again. After the windshield was gone, there would be only one probability to worry about. No other necessary conditions. No multiplication. Just one thing. Just the probability of my friend being killed before he could kill the shooter.

But the windshield stood.

When he told me the story later, he was sheepish. He laughed at himself. He was surprised he wanted the windshield out of the way.

He was surprised his training had gone so deep.

But deep training is another way to lower the risk of a bad thing happening.

The myth of the Border Patrol is that they care most about your documents.

They look closely at your passport when you approach the window. They compare your face to the face on the passport. They look at your supporting documents, like an airline ticket. If you go into secondary, they look at your receipts and electronic trail, too.

But documents can be faked.

Documents can be forged. Documents can be altered. Documents can be false. Plus, the Border Patrol has machines to tell them when documents are fake. If it was a simple document check, a robot could do it.

Instead, Border Patrol officers care about something more than your documents: They care about your behavior.

The next time you go through passport control, watch when the Border Patrol agent first looks at you. It's usually when you're still two or three back in line. That's when they do a first pass at your demeanor. They scan you for anything out of the ordinary. Nervousness. Discomfort. Agitation.

But most of all, they look for fear.

When fear hits, it's hard to stay still. Fear spikes your heartrate. Fear gets your blood pumping. Fear sends adrenaline through your body, so you can fight or run away.

If you're stuck in line or in a train seat, you get agitated. You shift around. You're nervous, because fear makes you want to move.

In the empty first-class train car, the Border Patrol had surrounded me, and it was on purpose. They could have sat in any of a hundred seats, but they didn't. They chose to surround me. One in front. One across the aisle, one behind me.

Being surrounded by the Border Patrol is a necessary condition of being arrested. It's a precursor. After they surround you, they can arrest you.

But being surrounded isn't a sufficient condition of arrest. Being surrounded doesn't mean they'll arrest you.

When the Border Patrol officer in front of me turned, I was nervous. I was agitated. Adrenaline from the sprint was mostly cooked off, but some was still in me. My heart rate was still elevated. I was a little flushed.

But I'd been trained for this moment. Trained to

____

not arouse suspicions. Trained to play my part.

I smiled at the Border Patrol officer and nodded.

He didn't nod back. Just stared at me.

I opened a book.

I looked at the pages and reminded myself to turn the page every 30 seconds. Because I wasn't reading. I was thinking.

I was thinking if I did something wrong. If I triggered a tripwire somewhere. If my sprint through the train station had brought focus on me. If there was some reason for them to arrest me.

I got ready for their questions. What I was doing. Where I was going. The purpose of my travels. None of which would be true.

I got ready to recite my alias's place of birth. My alias's birthday. My alias's previous travel. None of which would be true.

The Border Patrol officers turned to each other and started chatting in the local language. They talked and laughed and I turned the pages on my book every 30 seconds.

The train manager came by. He said something to the Border Patrol officers that I didn't catch, and they laughed some more. I offered my ticket to him, but since he was the one who sold it to me, he waved it away.

After a while, I put the book down and pretended to take a nap against the roller bag in the seat next to me.

For two more hours, the Border Patrol sat around me. If one of them got up to go to the bathroom, the other two stayed.

When we neared my destination, I got ready again to answer their questions. Because if they were going to stop me, this was where it would be.

I stood up and nodded again to the Border Patrol officer in front of me. He moved his legs out of the aisle. The Border patrol officer across the aisle made room, and the one behind me let me pass.

I waited at the door for the train to stop and got ready to answer their questions again. Because if they were going to stop me, they would first let me go. Then, they'd come up and want to talk. They'd want to let me think I was free, to see my reaction when they stopped me again.

But they didn't.

I got off the train and rolled my bag off the platform and into the train station. Inside, I found a bathroom. I went into a stall and thought about what to do.

It was strange what the Border Patrol officers had done.

Why sit in the seats surrounding me, when the rest of the first-class car was empty?

Why stay there the whole time, instead of moving around the train? Why leave at least two of them with me the whole time?

It was strange.

Strange enough I had to wonder if their job was to keep me surrounded until someone else came to arrest me. Maybe their job was to watch me until someone else higher up came. Maybe some counterintelligence agency was waiting for me at the second train station.

____

But no one had stopped me on the way to the bathroom. No one had arrested me.

But there was another possibility: They could be delaying the arrest until they saw who I met with. They could be trying to expose my source.

If so, they probably wouldn't have had uniformed Border Patrol officers on me. They would have preferred a plainclothes policeman, so I wouldn't be spooked.

But sometimes, the resources aren't there. And sometimes, orders get garbled. Maybe they didn't have any plainclothes policemen ready. And maybe the Border Patrol had been told to watch me but missed the part about doing it inconspicuously.

Which meant it was still possible I was under surveillance.

If I was under surveillance, I needed to know. I needed to know so I wouldn't expose the source.

I needed to take the risk of surveillance to zero.

There was nothing I could do in the train station to see if I was being surveilled. Inside the train station were no chokepoints. A surveillance team could set up static surveillance or back off and use the cameras.

To detect surveillance, I had to leave the train station. But I didn't have time for that.

Leaving the train station would mean missing the train to the town where I would meet the source.

Which meant I had to balance two risks:

1. The risk I was under surveillance and would get arrested (risk of a bad thing); and

2. The risk I'd miss the meeting (risk of good thing not happening)

And time was running out. Because my original plan was a bad plan.

The bad plan had been this:

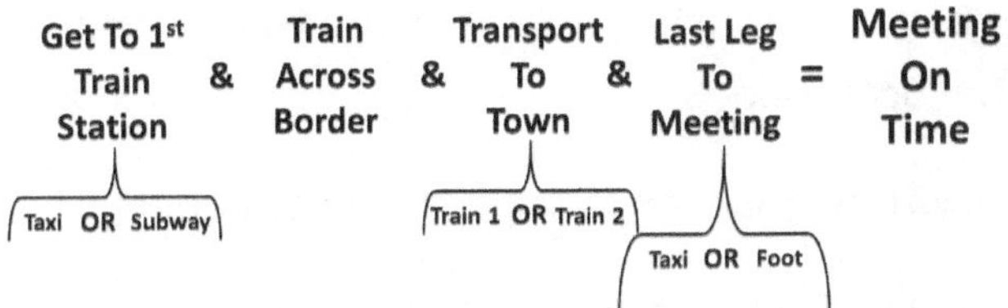

Taking the train across the border had been a single point of failure.

But everywhere else, I had choices.

To get to the destination town, I had a choice of two trains.

One train was the express train, direct to my destination, which is what I had planned to take. The other was the local train, much slower, with lots of stops before my destination.

I bought a ticket for the local train.

With the local train's stops, a surveillance team wouldn't know which town was my destination. Which meant they couldn't set up ahead of me. Which meant they'd need to have eyes on me at every stop.

At every stop, I'd have an opportunity to see them.

After buying the ticket, I went to the train platform for the local train.

That's where another strange thing happened.

A man was sitting, reading a newspaper. He was middle-aged, with just a briefcase. No overnight bag or coat. Just a newspaper and a briefcase.

After scanning his face in case I saw him again later, I turned my back to him.

I was now facing a reflective placard. In the reflection, I saw the man put down his newspaper and look me up and down, like he was committing me to memory.

I turned back around, and he raised his newspaper to cover his face.

He had looked at me without wanting me to know he was looking at me. Which was strange.

But there are lots of reasons for someone to do that. He might have liked my coat. He might have liked my roller bag. He might have liked me. Or I could have resembled someone he knew. Lots of reasons for someone to do that without being a surveillant.

Or, he could be a surveillant. Even though surveillants usually aren't so obvious about it. Especially in a train station where they can watch cameras remotely.

Or, he could be a surveillant but not surveilling me.

It happens, sometimes, because there are only so many chokepoints in each city. There are only so many transportation hubs. Only so many places where a spy, or anyone else the authorities want to follow, will go. Which means there are only so many places surveillants will be.

If you're ever with a spy in a foreign capital, ask them to show you where a spy would go to see if surveillance is on them.

They'll take you to a chokepoint.

On that day, a spy may be there. If he is, you won't notice him. Because he'll look like everyone else. He'll blend in.

Except for one thing: He'll be aware. More aware than everyone else. Hyperaware. He'll be looking at

---

everyone differently. At his surroundings differently. At the world differently. Which means you might pick him out if you see he's aware. But if he's good, you won't see he's aware, either.

What you'll see is his surveillance. You'll see the teams of five or six switching eyes on the target. You'll see them scurrying down side streets to get ahead. You'll see them sitting at a café table facing two intersections. You'll see them wait. Maybe, they'll adjust an earpiece. Maybe, they won't.

You'll see a minivan pull up and three unrelated people jump out. An old lady. A young man. A woman of different ethnicity. You'll see a nod from the guy at the café table. You'll see the others fan out to different corners.

You'll see them stop suddenly. You'll see them start again. You'll see their starts and stops aren't like the starts and stops of everyone else.

You'll see surveillants are the opposite of a spy. They're not aware of their surroundings. They're oblivious to the people around them. Because they don't need to be. They're the hunters, not the prey.

Ask the spy you're with to point them out. If you're feeling daring, follow them for a couple of streets. Maybe, you'll see the spy they're following. But probably not.

Because if the spy is good, he's already seen the surveillance. He knows he's being followed. Which means he'll act like everyone else. He'll blend in.

Which is what I was trying to do. I was trying to look like all the other travelers, tired and haggard. Which was easy after a taxi accident and sprint through the train station and the stress of being surrounded by the Border Patrol.

But there was still the possibility that surveillance was on me.

I needed to take the probability of surveillance to zero.

Like a fireman at a fire, it was time to remove a necessary condition of the risk.

The thirteen days in October 1962 that nearly triggered nuclear war are called the "Cuban Missile Crisis" in the United States. In Cuba, they're called the "October Crisis." In Russia, they could have been called the "Turkish Missile Crisis."

Before the crisis, the United States placed nuclear missiles with NATO allies. Nuclear missiles were in Great Britain. Nuclear missiles were in Italy. But the nuclear missiles that really bothered the Soviets were the Jupiter missiles in Turkey.

The Jupiter missiles in Turkey were above ground and vulnerable to attack. In the game theoretic logic of the Cold War, the Jupiter missiles couldn't be used as a deterrent, since they would be destroyed immediately if war began. And they could reach Moscow more quickly than other missiles. The Soviets looked at those facts and surmised the Jupiter missiles had only one purpose: A nuclear first strike.

A nuclear first strike would mean the Soviets would lose some of their command and control structure. Plus, many civilians would die. Most people in Moscow wouldn't have enough time to reach a nuclear shelter before the Jupiter missiles struck. A nuclear first strike would be catastrophic. It was the Soviets' worst fear. It was the risk that kept them up at night.

The Soviets started thinking about how to remove that risk.

The Soviets couldn't attack Turkey and remove the Jupiter missiles without triggering World War III, so they decided to reciprocate against the U.S. They started putting nuclear missiles in Cuba. Then, both sides would have missiles on each other's doorstep.

When the Kennedy Administration learned nuclear missiles were on the way to Cuba, there was panic. Beyond the strategic considerations, the political environment for the Kennedy administration meant Soviet missiles 90 miles off the U.S. coast was the worst thing possible.

Over more than a week of brinksmanship and negotiations in October 1962 that nearly tipped into nuclear war, a deal was hammered out between the U.S. and the Soviets.

The deal was this: The Soviets agreed to remove

---

their missiles from Cuba, and the United States would make a public promise to not invade Cuba.

But there was another part to the agreement.

A secret part.

The secret part wasn't discovered by most Americans until the late 1980s: The U.S. agreed to remove the Jupiter missiles from Turkey.

The Kennedy Administration didn't publicize that part. But removing the missiles from Turkey was the key to ending the Cuban Missile Crisis.

Before putting the Jupiter missiles in Turkey, U.S. strategists didn't look at the risks the way the Soviets did. They didn't see the Jupiter missiles in Turkey as a necessary condition of the worst risk the Soviets faced.

U.S. strategists didn't see the risk they created until the Soviets moved nuclear missiles to Cuba. Then, they saw the risk the way the Soviets saw it.

Then, they, like all strategists, obsessed over removing the necessary condition. They wanted to take the risk to zero.

They wanted to take the risk to zero of a first strike
that they couldn't respond to. They wanted the
missiles off their doorstep.

Good strategists reason backward from a risk to its
necessary conditions.

They take away a necessary condition of a risk to
reduce the risk to zero.

It's the same thing firefighters do: Take away the
necessary condition of heat, oxygen or fuel, and the
fire can't exist.

It's the same thing spies do: Remove the necessary
condition of a risk, and the risk can't exist.

4

Structuring Risks

To continuously track you, a surveillance team must follow you the whole time.

Which means you can take them wherever you want to take them.

You can take them through chokepoints and transportation changes. You can take them through open fields and crowded city streets. You can take them through hedgerows and alleyways. You can take them wherever you want to take them.

Wherever you take them, you have a chance to spot them.

If they had picked me up at the first train station, they could have surveilled me since. There were only two necessary conditions: In the train and in the second train station.

The Border Patrol had eyes on me while I was in the train. And they could have used cameras at the second train station.

If the intention was to surveil me, their capability to do it was one hundred percent for each necessary condition. One hundred percent multiplied by one hundred percent is one hundred percent.

As I sat on the local train, it was 100 percent that the security services could have watched me since the first train station.

It was time to lower their odds.

Taking the local train was the first step.

Since they didn't know where I was going, they'd need a surveillance team on the local train. But that wasn't a difficult test. If they were good, they could do it without me seeing them. The chance they could blend in with the rest of the passengers and get on without me seeing them: 80 percent.

Eighty percent is high. Which meant I had to create more conditions.

The next thing I did was move three cars up in the train. If they wanted to keep eyes on me, they would need to:

1. Follow me through the train; or

2. Have someone already in the cars ahead.

No one followed me through the train cars. And no one reacted, that I could see.

But if they were good, they would let me go through the train without following me. Maybe a 90 percent chance they did.

Overall odds were down to 72 percent, but that was still too high.

The next thing I did was get off the train at the third stop. I stood on the platform and waited for everyone to get off and on the train. There were no hesitations either way. No stops and starts. Nobody got off, looked at me and changed their mind.

When the conductor stuck his head out to blow his

----

whistle, I got back on the train.

That was a more difficult test to pass. If they were following me, maybe a 40 percent chance they could still follow me on and off the train without me seeing them.

Since getting on the local train, there were three necessary conditions. Seventy-two percent odds they passed the first two. And the third had taken it down to 28.8 percent that I was still being followed and hadn't seen the surveillance team.

Which was still too high.

Before I went to the meeting with the sensitive source, the probability that I was being followed without seeing surveillance had to be zero.

When you're taking risks, you're not passive. You're active.

You add layers of low-probability necessary conditions to lower the risk of a bad thing happening.

Closing in on the destination on the local train, the chance a surveillance team was on me and I hadn't seen them was still 28.8 percent.

Still too high.

Too high because 28.8 percent is higher than zero.

It had to be zero because the fallout from being caught with the sensitive source would be enormous. My face and his face would be all over the newspapers. The cost to diplomatic relationships would be astronomical. And espionage is still a capital offense in some places.

Before I went to the meeting, the chance I was being followed had to be zero. It had to be impossible for them to follow me without me seeing them.

Which meant I had to do one more thing.

When you could be surveilled, you're creating necessary conditions for the other side. You're taking the surveillance team through places where they need to get close to follow you. You're taking them through chokepoints where they need to get close or lose you.

Earlier in the day, I had done that.

I'd taken the probability down to zero by what I'd done in the earlier city.

But having the Border Patrol surround me had changed the calculation. And seeing the guy in the second train station look me up and down meant I had to drive the probability down to zero again.

And I didn't have much time.

Taking the local train instead of the express train had made time shorter. When the local train pulled into the town before my destination, I had thirty-five minutes before the meeting.

Enough time to introduce one more leg of travel.

I left the train station and jumped in a taxi.

The taxi driver was more what you'd expect from a taxi driver. He was settled in and relaxed. His body was molded to the seat. Most importantly, he didn't ask why I wanted to take a taxi to the next town, when I could have stayed on the train. And he didn't ask why I wanted my roller bag with me in the backseat instead of in the trunk.

He just flipped off his availability sign and took off.

I turned and watched to see if anyone followed us out of the train station.

No one did.

And no one followed us for the twenty-minute ride to the next town.

But a surveillance team could have caught the taxi number and asked the taxi company to tell them where I was dropped off. It was a low chance. Maybe, 10 percent.

But 10 percent is higher than zero. Which meant it was too high.

I told the taxi driver to drop me off away from the meeting site.

Away from the meeting site so if the security

services had the taxi company tell them where I had been dropped off, they still couldn't find me.

By the time I paid the taxi driver, it was 14 minutes before the meeting.

I started walking, trailing the roller bag behind me. I thought I was walking toward the meeting site, but I got turned around.

I got mixed up. I got lost because I hadn't planned for this. I hadn't planned to be walking in this part of a new town 8 minutes before the meeting.

By the time I figured out where I was, I was too far away to make it on time on foot.

After a day of travel, I was going to miss the meeting. After a day of risks, I was going to get nothing.

Then, I saw a taxi stand.

I ran toward it and jumped in the first taxi in line.

The driver asked for my destination. I told him.

He said, "It's too close."

Too close? I repeated. What do you mean, 'too close?'

"Find another taxi," he said.

With only a few minutes before the meeting, I didn't have time to argue. I got out and got in the second taxi in line.

The new taxi driver turned to me and said, "Why didn't you take that taxi?"

I said, He said where I want to go is too close.

The new taxi driver unbuckled his seatbelt and opened his door. "The rules are that he must take you."

I said, I need to go right away. Let's go.

But the new taxi driver was already outside his taxi and at the window of the first taxi driver and yelling at him.

I had only six minutes until the meeting. Now, two taxi drivers were yelling at each other about the rules of taxi stands.

———————————————————

Fortunately, the argument was short. Shorter than after the taxi crash earlier in the day.

The new taxi driver got back in the taxi and took me the five minutes to the meeting location.

Which gave me one minute to get ready for the meeting.

A meeting with a volatile guy.

A guy who almost killed his boss.

I had met this source before. In an earlier meeting, he started by saying, "I have a confession to make."

Which is not a good way to open a conversation with a spy.

Ok, I said. Go ahead.

He said, "My boss demoted me. He shamed me in front of the group. He is telling everyone behind my back that I should leave."

All of this I knew already, but I didn't interrupt.

He continued, "I was pulling my car onto the street, and my boss walked in front of me. It was - how do you say it in English? Serendipitous? Is that right?"

I don't know if that's the right word until you tell me what happened, I said. What happened?

"It was serendipitous," he continued. "It was a great opportunity."

At that moment, adrenaline spiked my system. My heartrate rose, and I looked away from the source. I looked at the walls and anything that could have a camera or a listening device. I looked through the windows to see if we were being watched. For any sign that I was going to be arrested.

Because if the source had been arrested for murder, one of the things he could have done is make a deal with the prosecutor. He could have negotiated to get a lighter sentence in exchange for flipping on me. In exchange for becoming a double agent. Maybe, the stuff he'd given me recently had all been planted by counterintelligence. Maybe, I was about to be arrested.

The source continued. "I could say that my foot slipped off the brake. Or the car suddenly accelerated." He paused and looked at me.

But you didn't? I said hopefully.

"No, I didn't," he said with regret. "I let him walk by. But maybe I shouldn't have. Maybe I should have taken the opportunity. Since then, it's only been worse."

But you didn't run him over? I asked again to confirm. You didn't kill your boss?

He looked at me like I wasn't listening. "No, of course, I didn't kill him," he said. "He's not worth it."

That was the guy I was trying to meet that first day in alias.

Before you become a spy, you think the hard part is the risk of bad things like surveillance, checkpoint attacks and enemies hunting you.

But when you become a spy, you learn that harder than preventing bad things is getting good things to happen.

Harder than being hunted is finding sources with access to secrets. Harder than making it through checkpoints is keeping sources motivated. Harder than avoiding surveillance is getting secrets out.

It's hard because good things have necessary conditions, too. Just like with bad things, taking away the necessary condition of a good thing means the good thing can't exist.

For intelligence, there are four necessary conditions for a source to be successful:

1. Access to secrets

2. Motivation to grab secrets

3. A way to get the secrets to you.

4. Enough savvy to not get caught.

It looks like this:

$$\frac{\text{Access \& Motivation \& Secrets Out \& Savvy}}{} = \text{Good Source}$$

It doesn't matter if they have access to secrets, if they have no way to get them to you. It doesn't matter if they're motivated to get secrets, if they don't have access. It doesn't matter if they have access, motivation and a way to get them to you if they're not savvy enough to not get caught. Because if they get caught and turned into a double-agent, you'll be fed bad intelligence. Which is worse than no intelligence at all.

Each one is a necessary condition; not even three together are sufficient to be a good source.

A source needs all four.

With good things, you're trying to keep all the necessary conditions. You're trying to make sure they all exist at the same time. You're trying to make sure all the necessary conditions exist and combine. So you get the effect.

To make a good thing happen, you're focused on all the necessary conditions. Instead of focusing on one necessary condition, you're focused on the whole bunch. You're trying to keep all of them alive.

Not just one. Not just two. All of the necessary conditions, however many there are.

When you find a source with all four necessary conditions of being a good source, great things can happen.

The source who met me that day had all four necessary conditions of a good source. He had access. He was motivated. He had a way to get the secrets to me. And he had enough savvy to not get caught, because he hadn't killed his boss.

When he arrived, he had no confessions to make.

He had no problems getting to the meeting site. No taxi crashes or suspected surveillance or taxi driver arguments. It had been smooth, he said.

Which meant we could get down to what he brought me.

It was something I wasn't expecting.

He pulled out a whole ream of documents. A lot of documents. More documents than he had ever brought me before.

And the quality was good. Very good. Higher quality than what he had ever brought me before.

There were documents that answered policymakers' questions. There were documents that plugged gaps in our intelligence collection. There were documents that, with other intelligence, would allow us to stop bad things from happening.

But there was a problem: He gave me too much.

He gave me more documents than I could safely secure. I hadn't expected that many, so I had no technical way to store them.

I couldn't cull them down. I couldn't get rid of any. I couldn't destroy any of the documents without losing valuable intelligence.

There were so many documents, they created a new risk.

A risk of being caught with all those documents on me.

To lower the risk, I needed to adjust my plan.

The source I met that day was one of many sources. One of many because I didn't know what was going to happen in the future.

I didn't know if Source A would have access to something important today. Or if Source B would. Or if a border conflict suddenly flared in Source C's territory.

I didn't know because I didn't know the future.

But I knew it was likely something would happen that Source A or Source B or Source C could report on. I knew that the chance of Source A or Source B or Source C producing intelligence in a certain time frame was high.

It was high because my simple model of intelligence production looked like this:

$$\textbf{Source A} \textbf{ OR } \textbf{Source B} \textbf{ OR } \textbf{Source C} \; = \; \textbf{Good Intelligence}$$

If Source A didn't produce anything, there was still Source B or Source C who could. If Source A and Source B didn't produce anything, Source C still could.

The OR operators were high in the model.

Which was important, because underneath the OR operators were lots of & operators. To produce intelligence, a lot of good things had to happen.

Under each source were the same four factors with & operators between them: Access, Motivation,

Ability to Get Secrets Out, and Savvy to not get caught.

It looks like this:

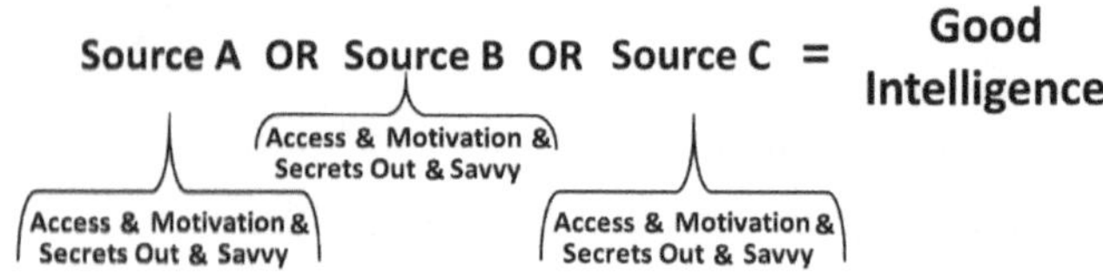

If you can keep each source independent of each other, the risks to each stay independent. Source A not producing intelligence didn't affect whether Sources B and C produced good intelligence. You only need one of your sources to produce good intelligence for you to get good intelligence.

To increase the chance of a good thing happening, you put lots of OR operators high in your model. You create lots of substitutes. You create lots of ways for the good thing to happen.

That day was the day that source produced good intelligence.

And it went beyond good. It was great. It was game-changing intelligence.

Now it was time to get it home.

With that many documents, it was the riskiest time on an already risky day.

I had no spy tools with me. Nothing clever made by a technician. No way to digitize them. No technical tools. No way to transmit the documents without carrying them.

With that many documents, it wouldn't take a full search to find them. Even a cursory look in my bag would be enough. If the security services stopped me, they would find the documents easily.

It was a riskier time than the taxi crash. Riskier than being surrounded by the Border Patrol. Riskier than meeting a volatile source.

A false passport and a cover story wouldn't save me anymore. If security services found the documents the source gave me, I couldn't talk my way out of it. The documents were sufficient for the security services to know I was a spy. There were no other necessary conditions. If they found me with the documents, they would know I was a spy.

To lower the risk, I went through the plan for the trip back one more time.

The plan had good chokepoints and good transportation changes and plenty of ways to detect surveillance. It had fallback transportation options if a train was delayed or a flight was missed or a taxi crashed.

The plan had lots of fallbacks because the trip back had no deadline. If I thought I might be under surveillance, I could extend my travel for days or weeks. I could substitute one transportation mode for another. I could add fallback after fallback, if necessary. I could take as long as needed to get back with the sensitive documents.

But I wanted to lower the risk of discovery even more, so I introduced one more OR operator, in case I found myself under surveillance.

If I was under surveillance, I'd need to get rid of the documents safely and securely. So they couldn't be tied to me. So they couldn't be traced back to the source.

To get rid of documents, one option is flushing them down a toilet. But flushing doesn't go quickly. And that many documents would probably clog the toilet.

A second option is burning. But that takes a while. And can leave fragments. Plus, fires make smoke, which attracts attention. If a surveillance team saw me burning something, they'd be on me before I burned page two.

So I created a third option: I walked into a hotel and grabbed two local newspapers.

Two local newspapers because the first one would be a decoy.

If I were under surveillance, the surveillance team would be watching for where I was going. They'd be watching for who I met next. And they'd also be watching for a brush pass or dead drop.

So I'd give them a dead drop. I'd drop the first newspaper somewhere they'd see it. Somewhere they'd zero-in. Somewhere they'd focus. Which would give me time to dispose of the second newspaper with the documents elsewhere.

It didn't take away all the risk. It didn't make the possible impossible. A surveillance team could still catch me with the documents, if they had enough people. If they decided to follow me after they saw a dead drop. If they caught me before I got rid of the documents in the second newspaper.

But the decoy dead drop added an OR operator to my side. And it added a couple more necessary conditions to their side. They'd need to follow me past the first dead drop & they'd need to catch me before the second dead drop.

The decoy dead drop lowered my risk of failure and raised a surveillance team's risk of failure at the same time.

The decoy dead drop made the possible less probable. But not impossible.

With that many documents, there was no way to

get risk to zero.

Which sometimes happens, when you're a spy.

Sometimes, you can't get the risk to zero.

Sometimes, you take the risk.

5

Taking Risks

With the documents wrapped in the second newspaper, I started home.

I followed the plan. The plan with the good chokepoints and good transportation changes and plenty of ways to detect surveillance. The plan with the fallback transportation options if a train was delayed or a flight was missed or a taxi crashed.

But the rest of that day, there were no more bad taxi drivers on amphetamines. No more car crashes. No more subway trains that made me late. No more Border Patrol officers surrounding me. No more strange watchers in a train station.

Which meant no need to add necessary conditions

to make a surveillance team expose themselves. No need for substitutes. No need for fallbacks or fallbacks on fallbacks. No need to change plans midstream.

No need for any of that.

There was no surveillance.

Everything was smooth.

Or so, I thought.

There's always the risk you're wrong. There's always the risk you made a mistake. There's always the risk you wanted something to be true, so you ignored contrary data.

It's the risk you were too invested in an outcome. It's the risk your analysis was biased, so you made bad decisions.

To mitigate that risk, I told my boss every step of what happened. Everything I saw. Everything I experienced. Everything I thought. Everything risk I took.

Because I wanted to know if I was wrong. I wanted to know if I made a mistake.

I wanted a second opinion.

A simple model is cause and effect.

Inside every model are two important things: Necessary conditions (separated by & operators) and substitutes (separated by OR operators).

The simplest way to lower risks is to remove a necessary condition. Remove a necessary condition, and the bad thing has a probability of zero.

A lot of the time, you can't do that. So instead, you layer on low-likelihood necessary conditions.

If you can't do that, you create fallbacks. So you can react to bad things before they get worse.

Making good things happen is the other side of risk. Good things happening are the reason we take the risk of bad things happening.

But making good things happen isn't easy.

For good things, there are also necessary conditions. There are also substitutes. To increase the chance of a good thing happening, we elevate the substitutes to the top level of simple models.

And we have substitutes for as many necessary conditions as possible.

It looks like this:

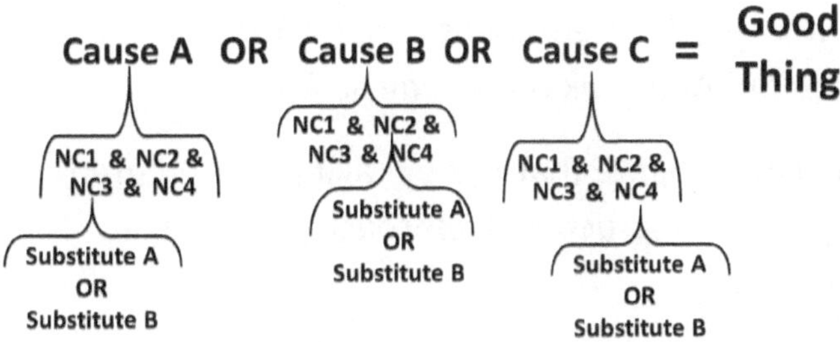

To increase the likelihood of good things:

1. Elevate OR operators as high in the model as possible by creating substitute causes of the good thing.

2. Where necessary conditions of a good thing exist, create more substitutes and backups and fallbacks.

But there's another risk that goes beyond good and

---

bad things when you're looking at risks: There's the risk you got it wrong.

There's the risk you misunderstood the necessary conditions of bad things. There's the risk that you got wrong the substitutes. There's the risk you filled in the model in the wrong way.

You could have the wrong data. You could have applied the wrong analytic framework. You could have everything else right, but still made a bad decision. And took the wrong action.

You can mitigate that risk by taking a structured approach. A structured approach gives you a checklist.

But you can't escape the risk that the model you used was wrong.

You can't take that risk to zero.

Because a model is not reality. A map is not the territory.

No matter how good you are at judging risks and how good your model is, there's always the risk your model and things in it are wrong.

But a structured approach gives you something

else: A vocabulary to get a second opinion.

When you get a second opinion, it helps to talk to someone who has done a similar thing before.

My boss was an experienced guy. He'd been in alias many times. He'd done it in dangerous places. He'd done it and been successful. He'd taken risks and managed risks and got the intelligence and survived.

I told him what happened. From the taxi accident to the Border Patrol to the man in the train station to my adjustments on the way.

He nodded. "And the trip back?"

Nothing happened, I said. It was smooth.

He nodded. "You're probably fine. Maybe you came across a surveillance team and they dropped you. They didn't stay with you to the meeting. And if they were going to arrest you, it would have been on the way back. Did you get anything good?"

It's very good, I said. And there's lots of it.

He nodded again. "Then it was worth it."

The intelligence went into the CIA's system. A system where analysts looked at it, sifted through it, and passed on higher what was valuable.

Some of it was very valuable. Some of it went to the highest levels.

The highest levels had follow-up questions. And a request for more intelligence like that. They wanted to use it to take actions affecting millions of people.

To get that day's intelligence, there had been a lot of necessary conditions. Some of them were low probability.

6

Summary

This little book is about taking risks. It's also about having the right analytic framework for thinking about risks.

If you'd like to learn more about risks, strategy and how to process quickly under pressure, join the email list at spysguide.com.

The simple framework in this book of necessary conditions and substitutes helps you work through risks in your head. Or on a sheet of paper.

It's a framework that forces you to be brutally honest about the causes of bad things happening. And the sufficient conditions of good things happening.

Using & and OR operators is a simple way to analyze risks.

But it's not the only model for risk.

If you're working with large numbers, there are better models for risk.

If you can collect lots of data and can spin the wheel many times, there are better models for risk.

If you have all the possibilities defined and can derive probabilities, there are better models for risk.

If you have lots of time and lots of chances and can recoup losses, there are better models for risk.

But when you're a spy, you're working with small numbers. You're working in a world where all the possibilities aren't defined. You're working where probabilities are difficult to get right. You're working where there isn't lots of time. There aren't lots of chances. And you can't recoup losses, because one failure can kill you.

In that world, you need a model you can carry in your head. A simple model of cause and effect.

A model you can use in a taxi, subway car and surrounded by the Border Patrol.

A model for taking risks you can use on the fly.
